Giraffes

By Mary Molly Shea

Gareth Stevens
Publishing

Please visit our Web site, www.garethstevens.com. For a free color catalog of all our high-quality books, call toll free 1-800-542-2595 or fax 1-877-542-2596.

Library of Congress Cataloging-in-Publication Data

Shea, Mary Molly.
 Giraffes / Mary Molly Shea.
   p. cm. – (Animals that live in the grasslands)
 Includes index.
 ISBN 978-1-4339-3867-2 (pbk.)
 ISBN 978-1-4339-3868-9 (6-pack)
 ISBN 978-1-4339-3866-5 (library binding)
 1. Giraffe—Juvenile literature. 2. Grassland animals—Juvenile literature. I. Title.
 QL737.U56S44 2011
 599.638—dc22
                                              2010000408

First Edition

Published in 2011 by
Gareth Stevens Publishing
111 East 14th Street, Suite 349
New York, NY 10003

Copyright © 2011 Gareth Stevens Publishing

Designer: Michael J. Flynn
Editor: Therese Shea

Photo credits: Cover, pp. 1, 5, 9 (both), 11 (both), 13, 15, 17, 19, back cover Shutterstock.com; p. 7 Tim Flach/Stone+/Getty Images; p. 21 Manoj Shah/Riser/ Getty Images.

Printed in the United States of America

CPSIA compliance information: Batch #CS10GS: For further information contact Gareth Stevens, New York, New York at 1-800-542-2595.

Table of Contents

Boldface words appear in the glossary.

Hello Up There!

Which animal can stand on the ground and look into your school's second floor? A giraffe! Giraffes are the tallest animals on Earth. They live in Africa's **grasslands**.

Bulls, Cows, and Calves

Male giraffes are called bulls. They can be as tall as three adults standing on each other! **Female** giraffes are called cows. They are a bit shorter than bulls.

Everything about a giraffe is big. A giraffe's hoof is about 12 inches (30 cm) wide. Its heart is twice as wide. A bull can weigh as much as a small car!

hoof

All giraffes have spots. Some have light brown spots. Some have darker spots. Many people think a giraffe's spots help it hide among trees.

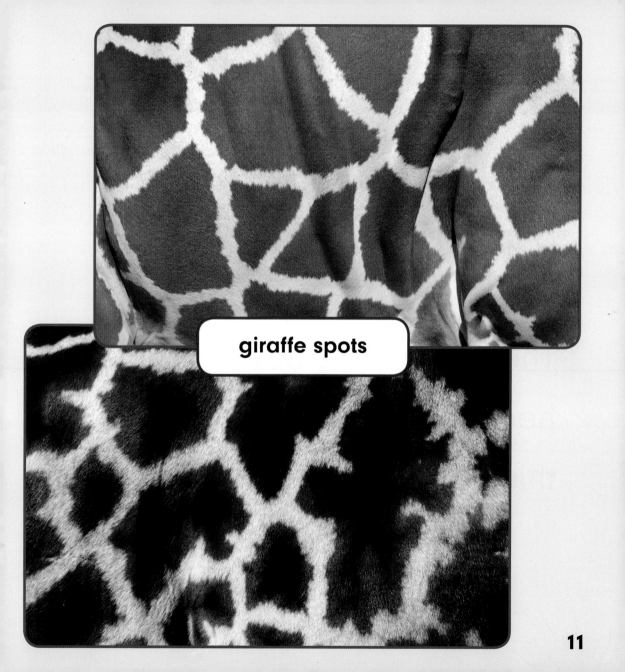

giraffe spots

11

Giraffes live in groups. They play and fight. They swing their necks at each other. They bump the **horns** on their heads. Bulls fight for **mates** in this way.

horns

A baby giraffe is called a calf. Calves are big, too. They are about 6 feet (1.8 m) tall when they are born. They begin to walk about 1 hour after they are born!

calf

Eating and Drinking

Giraffes eat a lot of leaves. A giraffe's long **tongue** can pull leaves off trees. It gets water from the leaves it eats.

tongue

Sometimes, giraffes drink water. First, they spread their front legs. Then, they bend their necks down to the water. One giraffe may watch for enemies while others drink.

Enemies

Lions and crocodiles are the only animals that hunt giraffes. Giraffes usually see them from far away. Giraffes can **protect** themselves. They run fast and kick hard!

Fast Facts

Height	bulls: about 18 feet (5.5 meters) cows: about 14 feet (4.3 meters) calves: about 6 feet (1.8 meters)
Weight	bulls: up to 3,000 pounds (1,360 kilograms) cows: up to 1,500 pounds (680 kilograms) calves: up to 150 pounds (70 kilograms)
Diet	leaves
Average life span	about 25 years in the wild

Glossary

female: a girl

grasslands: land on which grass is the main kind of plant life

horn: a hard growth on an animal's head

male: a boy

mate: one of a pair of animals that come together to make a baby

protect: to guard

tongue: the body part inside a mouth used for tasting, licking, and eating

For More Information

Books

Anderson, Jill. *Giraffes*. Minnetonka, MN: NorthWord Books for Young Readers, 2005.

Bodden, Valerie. *Giraffes*. Mankato, MN: Creative Education, 2009.

Ufer, David. *The Giraffe Who Was Afraid of Heights*. Mount Pleasant, SC: Sylvan Dell Publishing, 2006.

Web Sites

African Wildlife Foundation: Giraffe
www.awf.org/content/wildlife/detail/giraffe
Read about how much a giraffe can eat each day as well as other fun facts.

San Diego Zoo's Animal Bytes: Giraffe
www.sandiegozoo.org/animalbytes/t-giraffe.html
See videos of giraffes in action.

Index

About the Author

Mary Molly Shea, a practicing nurse and forensic scientist, spends her free time rescuing animals in western New York and doing research for books like this one.